Little Pebble

Habitats

All About
Mountains

by Christina Mia Gardeski

CAPSTONE PRESS
a capstone imprint

Little Pebble is published by Capstone Press,
1710 Roe Crest Drive, North Mankato, Minnesota 56003
www.mycapstone.com

Library of Congress Cataloging-in-Publication Data
Names: Gardeski, Christina Mia, author.
Title: All about mountains / by Christina Mia Gardeski.
Description: North Mankato, Minnesota : Capstone Press, 2018. |
    Series: Little pebble. Habitats
Identifiers: LCCN 2017031567 (print) | LCCN 2017033060 (ebook) |
    ISBN 9781515797685 (eBook PDF) | ISBN 9781515797548 (hardcover) |
    ISBN 9781515797609 (paperback)
Subjects: LCSH: Mountains—Juvenile literature. | Mountain ecology—Juvenile literature.
Classification: LCC GB512 (ebook) | LCC GB512 .G37 2018 (print) |
    DDC 577.5/3—dc23
LC record available at https://lccn.loc.gov/2017031567

Editorial Credits
Marissa Kirkman, editor; Juliette Peters (cover) and Charmaine Whitman (interior), designers;
Eric Gohl, media researcher; Katy LaVigne, production specialist

Photo Credits
Getty Images: Minden Pictures/Sumio Harada, 18, Roberta Olenick, 21; Shutterstock: Andrij Vatsyk, cover, Dave Allen Photography, 9 (top), Dennis W Donohue, 12, Dmitry Pichugin, 11, Ekaterina Kuchina, 15, fedir13, back cover, interior (mountains illustration), FloridaStock, 20, Jakl Lubos, 7, Jon Bilous, 1, karamysh, 5, megmarie117, 17, Michal_K, 13, Vitalfoto, 19, Volodymyr Burdiak, 9 (bottom), welcomia, 10

Printed and bound in the USA.
629

Table of Contents

What Is a Mountain?. 4

The Bottom 10

The Top 14

Glossary 22
Read More 23
Internet Sites 23
Index 24

What Is a Mountain?

A mountain is a high land.

It is made of rock.

A mountain can be steep.

Its peak can be sharp.

peak

Some peaks are round.

Others are flat.

round peak

flat peak

The Bottom

Forests grow at the base.

Rivers flow.

This habitat is full of life.

base

Bears catch fish.

Mountain lions hunt.

mountain lion

The Top

It is cold at the peak.

Snow falls.

15

There is less oxygen.

Few trees grow.

Few animals can live here.

Mountain goats climb.

They grip with strong hooves.

hooves

Eagles nest in cliffs.

They spy on the world below.

Glossary

base—the bottom of a mountain

eagle—a large bird with strong eyes and powerful wings that can nest in the cliffs of a mountain

habitat—the home of a plant or animal

hoof—a part of the foot of some animals that is made of horn and protects its toes

mountain goat—a hooved mountain animal with a beard, a short tail, and curved black horns

mountain lion—a large, powerful wild cat that lives in the mountains

oxygen—a tasteless, odorless gas needed to breathe

peak—the top of a mountain

steep—having a very sharp slope up and down

Read More

Arnold, Quinn M. *Mountains*. Seedlings. Mankato, Minn.: Creative Education, 2017.

Magby, Meryl. *Mountain Goats*. American Animals. New York: PowerKids Press, 2014.

Royston, Angela. *Mountain Food Chains*. Food Chains and Webs. Chicago: Heinemann Library, 2015.

Internet Sites

Use FactHound to find Internet sites related to this book.

Visit www.facthound.com

Just type in 9781515797548 and go.

Check out projects, games and lots more at
www.capstonekids.com

Index

bases, 10
bears, 12

eagles, 20

forests, 10

hooves, 18

mountain goats, 18
mountain lions, 12

oxygen, 16

peaks, 6, 8, 14

rivers, 10
rocks, 4

snow, 14

trees, 16